The Adventures of Jason and the Argonauts

A play freely adapted from the ancient myths

Phil Willmott

Samuel French — London
www.samuelfrench-london.co.uk

THE ADVENTURES OF JASON AND THE ARGONAUTS

First performed at the Scoop open-air Amphitheatre, More London Riverside, SE1 2DB on August 5th 2009 with the following cast:

King Pelias	Raymond Coker
Medea	Siobhan O'Kelly
Storyteller	Ursula Mohan
Jason	Joe Fredericks
Chiron the Centaur	Richard Franklin
Hera as a hag	Paddy Crawley
Princess Creusa/the Goddess Hera	Lauren Storer
Argonaut Narcissus	Christopher Hogben
Argonaut Hercules	Paddy Crawley
Argonaut Castor	Jamie Menard
Argonaut Pollux	Matthew Grace
Argonaut Atlanta	Joanna Woodward
Argrin the Boat Builder	Richard Franklin
Argonaut Cat/the Goddess Artemis	Briony Price
Lascivious Gatekeeper/ Crone of Lemnos	Ursula Mohan
Queen Callisto of Lemnos	Briony Price
Colchis Fishwife	Ursula Mohan
King Aeetes of Colchis	Richard Franklin
The Great Bull of Colchis	Raymond Coker
Dragon Snake	Christopher Hogben

Directed by Phil Willmott
Produced by Suzanna Rosenthal for The Steam Industry

COPYRIGHT INFORMATION

(See also page ii)

CHARACTERS

King Pelias
Medea
Story Teller (male or female)
Jason
Chiron the Centaur
Hera as a hag (male)
Princess Creusa/the Goddess Hera
Male Argonaut Narcissus
Male Argonaut Hercules
Male Argonaut Castor
Male Argonaut Pollux
Female Argonaut Atlanta
Male or Female Argonaut Argrin
Female Argonaut Cat/the Goddess Artemis
Lascivious Crone
Queen Callisto
King Aeetes of Colchis
Colchis Fishwife
The Great Bull of Colchis
Male or female Dragon Snake
Additional Argonauts

The action of the play takes place in a city square

Costumes: Ancient Greece (with a few fun twists)

PREFACE

This script is a record of how the piece was originally performed in 2009 but I hope directors will feel free to make it funny and relevant to their own audience and to adapt the staging to make best use of their resources.

The tale is told by a group of travelling players in a town square so you only really need the type of simple props that can be pulled out of a prop basket. Additionally the original production had some big, elaborate puppets for Chiron the Centaur, the Bull of Colchis and the Dragon Snake. If you have some money I suggest you too spend it on these elements but if not you can just as easily represent the beasts with actors in masks. Try to get a beautiful model ship for the clashing rock sequence though, if you can.

Please feel free to update the topical references to film stars and TV programmes and several of the characters, notably the ship's cat, speak in youthful street language which dates very quickly so you may need to update this too.

You can present the piece as a play with minimal music, just including a pop song for Narcissus and a song at the end, or you can incorporate more numbers if you like. We used the Katrina and the Waves song *Walking on Sunshine* when Jason was training, reprising the tune in a tense arrangement as underscoring for the Clashing Rocks sequence and for a big sing-along finale. Perhaps you could use Bonnie Tyler's *Holding Out For A Hero*, sung by backing singers, when Jason strips and carries Hag Hera across the water. Our harpies sang Gloria Gaynor's *I Will Survive* and Narcissus charmed them with *Hero* by Enrique Iglesias. You may have better ideas. Twinkly celestial percussion can also usefully underscore the goddesses.

If you'd like to present the show as a two act, full-scale musical the lyricist Kenny Wax and composer Geoff Morrow have written a complete set of catchy songs you can insert. Details are available via www.kennywax. com. Although time constraints meant I eventually used very little of their music it was Kenny who first alerted me to the potential of putting Jason's quest on stage.

However you choose to incorporate songs please note the appendix at the back of this script entitled Use of Copyright Music. If you're using pop songs and you can't manage a live band there are some excellent karaoke accompaniments available that you can sing along to.

Finally, although the show works very well on its own, we presented this comedy as the first half of a double bill. Later that evening the same actors performed the ancient Greek tragedy *Medea*, Euripides' dramatic account of the terrible events which befell Jason and Medea later in life. I'd recommend this to any particularly ambitious producer as it proved a fantastic way of introducing a new audience to Greek tragedy and the actors loved the workout performing the contrasting pieces gave them.

However you choose to present *The Adventures of Jason and the Argonauts* good luck, I hope you have fun. We had a great time.

Phil Willmott

For Ursula Mohan

This brilliant actress and teacher, who inspired thousands of young actors during her time coaching at the Arts Educational School, inspired us with a hilarious performance as the crones in *Jason* followed by a heart wrenching portrayal of the nurse in *Medea*.

The Adventures of Jason and the Argonauts

A city square

Herald (*announcing*) His Majesty King Pelias, supreme ruler of all Greece!

During the following speech, the Argonauts — disguised as travelling players — enter the town square. One of them "Robbie" is carrying a recorder

King Pelias (*addressing the audience as if they were his subjects*) Citizens of Athens, my people, (*with distaste*) little children, it is seven weeks to the day since my upstart nephew Jason stood before me here and accused me of murdering his father, my own brother. (*Pause*) You know me as a fair man. Rather than have his guts strung around this square as festival decorations, I decided to let the gods decide his fate and sent him on a quest. His challenge was to fetch the Golden Fleece from a distant land far beyond the horizon, a mythical prize guarded by every kind of monster, temptation and peril. If he could return by twilight this evening, I promised to step aside and declare him King in my place. (*Pause*) It is an hour until the time allotted for his return and I can reassure those of you who love me, your rightful ruler, that there have been no sightings of the snotty little brat. (*Pause*) The gods have sent us a clear message; the hurtful things he accused me of were all lies, and somewhere out there he has suffered a cruel death as punishment for his falsehoods. (*Pause*) Let the celebrations commence. Unicorn pie will be served to all on the steps of the palace at nineteen hundred hours and two hundred virgins will be sacrificed in the town square at midnight.

Herald May the gods protect King Pelias the great.

Medea (*in disguise; addressing the King*) Your Majesty!

King Pelias Ah, volunteering for the virgin sacrifice? Splendid. Sign up round the back.

Medea (*ignoring him*) Your Majesty, may my little theatre troop be first to congratulate you on your defeat of Jason.

Disguised Argonauts All hail King Smelly Arse!

King Pelias It's Pelias!

Medea Forgive our ignorance, your Majesty. We are a group of travelling players, actors from across the sea who make our living by roaming from island to island performing stories of bravery and valour to entertain the crowds.

King Pelias Could you do *Phantom of the Amphitheatre?* I like that one.

Medea Alas, that is not in our repertoire. But we have heard news of your nephew Jason on our travels, and could enact his recent adventures for your entertainment.

King Pelias He comes to a grizzly end, right? I mean you're not going to spring a happy ending on me?

Medea Our story ends with Jason staring into the mouth of the gigantic Dragon Snake that guards the Golden Fleece. No man has ever escaped the vicious monster.

King Pelias Splendid! Splendid! What fun. I'm sure we'd love to see your little play. Songs by Andrewsus Lloyd Webbercus?

Medea No, Majesty. But we do have Robbie and his recorder!

Robbie steps forward and gives his recorder a rather pathetic trill

King Pelias (*unimpressed*) Oh… (*Excited again*) But there'll be lots of multi-million pound special effects, right? To conjure up all the monsters and battles and violence in the story.

Medea We've got some really cool puppets.

King Pelias (*dangerously unimpressed*) Is it short?

Medea Time will fly on Mercury's wings, Sire.

King Pelias Well, we've got an hour till the pie's ready. Can you fit your little show into an hour or so?

Medea The sooner we begin…

King Pelias Oh, very well, I don't suppose they've rounded up enough virgins yet. You may commence. (*He settles on his throne to watch*)

Medea Ladies and Gentlemen, Boys and Girls, Great Ones of Athens. May I introduce our storyteller...

The company present the Storyteller

Amidst much clatter of percussion

Storyteller   Oh, for a muse of fire that would ascend
                   My feeble powers of narration!
                   All Greece for a stage, real princes to act,
                   And actual ships to ride the swelling seas!
                   What if young Jason, could *himself* appear,
                   Strap on a sword and armour here,

With (as fierce and loyal as hounds)
His friends the *actual* Argonauts?
They'd win much glory with this tale.
Suppose, within the girdle of our stage,
You see two teenagers meet, young Jason
And sweet Medea, a newcomer to Greece.

Jason and Medea are sulky inexpressive teens at this point

Medea All right?
Jason All right.

Medea can't suppress her energy for much longer. Jason still trying to remain cool

Medea My father sent me here to keep me out of trouble.
Jason Can you use a bow and arrow?
Medea Yes.
Jason Know any jokes?
Medea Yes.
Jason (*shrugging*) Cool.
Storyteller   Piece out our imperfections with your thoughts.
                        Think, when I talk of centaurs, that you see one
                        Printing his proud hoofs i' th' receiving earth.
                        For 'tis your thoughts that now must deck our kings,
                        Carry them here and there, jumping o'er times.

Chiron the Centaur appears. Chiron is a crotchety, professor type

Jason Who are you? What are you?
Chiron I am Chiron, a centaur. Half man and half horse seeing as you ask. Impudent boy! And you had best learn some manners. I have news for you — you are not who you think you are!
Jason You mean... You mean... I've got the X factor?!
Chiron Certainly not... Well, maybe... No. I bring news of much greater importance. You were stolen away from the palace as a baby. Your true father was a ruler here. You are the rightful king of Athens.
King Pelias (*interrupting the action from his throne from where he watches*) Funny! This play's so funny! (*To Medea*) You were right, virgin. This is most amusing.
Chiron (*back to the play*) Do you realize what that means?
Jason Of course — no more chores and homework.
Chiron Foolish boy, my news has greater significance. Your father

was murdered by his jealous brother Pelias. The younger brother has seized the throne and all Greece suffers under his cruel tyranny. It is your destiny to challenge the tyrant and take your place as rightful king.

King Pelias (*warning the actors*) Be very careful.

The actors bow to Pelias as if submissively

Jason Challenge a king, me? But I don't know ——
Chiron Precisely, you don't know anything. This is why we need to begin your training. Now, do you have some lusty youth to train alongside you for moral support?
Jason There's Medea?
Chiron A girl!
Jason But she's as brave and strong as any boy.
Medea And a lot brighter too.
Chiron That wouldn't be too difficult.

Jason starts to exercise like a boxer. Appropriate training music starts

Pay attention young Jason, work hard and we'll make a hero of you yet. (*He moves to one side*)

The Storyteller takes the stage once more

Storyteller   With schooling all completed,
                       The centaur satisfied,
                       He leaves to claim his father's throne ——
Medea   — Medea at his side.

Training montage and boxing music finishes

Storyteller   Dare he rouse the spiteful king,
                       Complete the centaur's plan?
                       All we need's an actor who
                       Can play this cruel man.

A very unassuming actor puts on a crown or a crown is given to a member of the audience

King Pelias (*indicating whoever's playing him*) Is that supposed to be me?
Storyteller I'm afraid he's the only actor available, Majesty.

King Pelias (*to the actor playing him*) Step aside! If anyone's going to play me in the movie it's going to be me. Unless?

Storyteller Yes Majesty?

King Pelias Tom Cruisicus isn't available, is he?

Storyteller No, Your Majesty.

King Pelais Then I suppose I must give reign to my thespian tendencies.

Storyteller A script, Your Majesty?

King Pelias I remember what I said. (*Stepping into the story*) So, young Jason. You expect me to give up my throne, just like that, based upon the lies of (*indicating Chiron the Centaur*) old horse chestnuts over there?

Jason I speak the truth. The gods will prove it so.

King Pelias Will they indeed? Personally I never trouble myself with the gods. *Songs of Praise* isn't my kind of tea time viewing.

Jason You doubt the gods?

King Pelias I don't bother them, they don't bother me. It's obvious they want me as king. Perhaps now is the time to test my theory. I challenge you to capture and bring home the Golden Fleece of Colchis!

The challenge is spoken against a drum beat. This can be performed "straight" or as a rap

As the speech continues the Herald shows the audience related pictures from a flip chart — a snake, the fleece, a piece of cake etc.

> If you're the man you say you are,
> I challenge you to journey far,
> Make across the mighty ocean,
> For distant Colchis, where a snake,
> A giant Dragon Snake in fact,
> Guards a precious artefact.
> They call this prize the Golden Fleece,
> Return with it in seven weeks
> And I'll hand back my crown to you.
> It sounds a simple thing to do,
> Yet many try and all have failed.
> You'll see as soon as you set sail,
> That many perils wait to snare
> The traveller so best beware.
> Babes who turn to vicious birds,
> There's crashing rocks too I have heard;
> A bull so fierce its breath is fire,

Skulls who fight and never tire.
And yet, no doubt, for heaven's sake,
You'll find all that a piece of cake!
A lad like you, in seven weeks,
Can easily fetch me that Fleece.
So hurry, boy, *auf wiedersehen.*
(*Aside*) We won't be seeing him again!

Storyteller And so Jason left the King's presence. A million questions reverberated around our young hero's mind, chief amongst them being ——

Jason and Medea are alone

Jason What's the Golden Fleece?

Medea (*don't you know anything reaction*) It's a sheepskin coat made from a magical ram that once belonged to Zeus, the king of the gods. One of your ancestors flew on its back to the distant land of Colchis where the ram was sacrificed to the sun god and its coat was hung in a sacred grove guarded by a Dragon Snake. (*Beat*) Weren't you paying attention at all in hero class?

Jason So I just have to fight a Dragon Snake? No problem.

Medea There's more to it than that, it's a long perilous sea voyage to Colchis and the king there believes he will lose his power if the fleece is ever stolen, so the grove is well protected.

Jason I'd better pack some sandwiches. Sounds like I won't be back till late.

Medea Jason, you have to plan this carefully! Colchis is a long boat journey away (*pointing out front*) beyond the horizon, beyond many uncharted islands, home to many strange creatures and customs. Now, what does your hero training teach you?

Jason Er… We'll need a boat?

Medea Brilliant!

Jason But May, we're broke!

Medea What does hero training tell us is more useful than cash?

Jason Credit cards?

Medea Friends!

Jason Oh yeah, well, I've got you.

Medea You have.

Jason And… and… we don't really know anyone else.

Medea That's the trouble with home schooling.

Hera (disguised as an old hag) enters with a tray of medicines

Hera (*calling out her wares*) Potions, cures and poultices, remedies and rhymes! Let Old Mother Superdrug cure what ails you! Potions, cures and poultices, remedies and rhymes! Get your potions, cures and poultices, remedies and rhymes, here.

Medea Hallo, old lady!

Hera Potions, cures and poultices, remedies and rhymes!

Medea We're in very good health.

Hera I tell fortunes too for two groats.

Jason We've only got half a groat.

Hera (*snatching it*) I'll take it! There's a recession on. Give me your hands. (*Standing between them hand in hand and incanting*)

> O mighty forces of Earth, Sea and Air,
> Spirits of fire, of pleasure and care,
> Give me the knowledge Athena forbids;
> What lies in store for these two crazy kids?

There is a thunder clap

Oh dear, oh dear, oh dear.

Jason Not good news?

Hera (*handing them merchandise from her tray*) Here, take some of my failsafe industrial strength ointment of cloves and some soothing sleeping balm for the forehead. You're going to need them.

Jason Really? Well, thank you er...?

Hera Old Mother Superdrug.

Jason Thank you, Old Mother Superdrug. But can you be more specific?

Hera The perils that await you should not be faced alone. You must win friends to help you.

Medea Win them?

Hera Quite so. Through kindness.

Jason I don't understand, is it like winning the lottery?

Hera Even better.

Jason Wow! Where can I buy a scratch card?

Hera You must show the world an act of selflessness. (*Slyly*) For instance...

Jason }
Medea } (*together*) Yes?

Hera Well, I need to get across the water, it's many days walk around it but... Well, you're a bit of a hunk... you could carry me across on your back, handsome?

Jason What do you think, May?

Medea The centaur taught us to do good deeds whenever possible and I can sprint around to the other side. Got your swimming trunks?
Jason Well, yes but…
Hera Strip!

Jason appears to carry Hera "piggy back". One of "her" legs can be thrown over Jason's shoulder while he stands with the other on a box behind him to take his weight. Jason mimes swimming with his arms

Storyteller As Jason strode out across the bay with the old lady on his back she seemed to grow heavier and heavier.
Hera Cheeky!
Storyteller But with diligence, dexterity and care he ensured she arrived on the opposite bank completely dry.
Hera (*indicating she's thirsty*) Actually, I am a bit parched.

Someone brings her a cup of tea

Thanks, love. (*Drinking it down and staring into the cup*) Ooh my word, look at these tea leaves, very suspicious configuration I must say. (*Incanting*) What can you tell us o mystic tea leaves? (*Holding the tea cup to her ear*) The leaves say… the leaves say… It is time for me to throw off my disguise and reveal my true identity! (*Straightening up and throwing off the disguise to reveal himself as a rather unconvincing beauty*) Behold. Feast your eyes upon my beauty as your just reward. It was me all along!
Jason I'm sorry have we me―――? Do we know each other?
Hera It is I…
Jason Er?
Storyteller Hera.
Jason Can't quite place…
Storyteller (*prompting him*) It's Hera, the beautiful goddess of women.
King Pelias (*interrupting again*) No wonder Jason doesn't recognize the goddess, that actor looks ridiculous. You need a looker in this role and I know just the beauty. Ladies and gentlemen, for one night only, in the role of the goddess Hera, my youngest daughter Alcestis.

Vampy music

A big entrance for Creusa, a real babe, who takes over the role of Hera amidst wolf whistles etc.

Hera (*incanting*)Mighty winds of North and South,
East Wind, West Wind roar about,
Make young Jason's crew appear,
Sweep them up and blow them here!

Jason covers up as a huge gust of wind blows the Argonauts, one by one, before Jason. First up is Narcissus. A swaggering pop star type

Narcissus (*checking out Hera*) Hey, who's the babe?!
Hera I am the goddess Hera.
Narcissus Why is it all the cuties are always taken or celestial deities?
Jason I'm Jason.
Narcissus Hey, always up for adventure, Bro. My name's Narcissus. Now I know what you're thinking — what's an A-list pop star doing taking time out from a busy career? Fair point Jase, the truth is me and my record company need a little time out too, know what I'm saying? So what better than a tour to get back to my roots, pick up some new vibes... meet some chicks. There's gonna be chicks where we're going, right?
Jason I'm sure.
Narcissus I'm on board if you'll have me, Jase.
Jason Glad to have you with us. Who's next?

Atlanta steps up. A hearty Wild West gal

Atlanta Howdy y'all, I'm Princess Atlanta. Yee-ha!
Narcissus Yee-ha! (*She slaps Jason on the back*)
Jason Yee...Oww!
Atlanta I hear you're looking for adventurers. My pa, Iasius, wanted a boy and left me out on Mount Olympus to be brought up by the animals — so I can hunt as hard as a grizzly bear, see as sharp as an eagle and fight as fierce as a mountain lion and did I mention I can sing like a coyote? I sure as heck ain't settlin' down to married life now pa's taken to fixin' me up with a husband. So I've run away and I'm happy to hitch up with you if you'll have me.
Jason Love to have you along.

Castor and Pollux arrive

Castor ⎫
Pollux ⎭ (*together*) Greetings, Captain Jason.
Castor We are the famous twins, Castor ——
Pollux — and Pollux.

Castor Side by side we fight bravely for injustice wherever we find it.

Pollux Identical in bravery, agility, guile and swordsmanship, the world cannot tell us apart.

Castor We also have a cool habit of being able to ——

Castor }
Pollux } (*together*) — finish each other's sentences.

Pollux Which can also be quite annoying depending ——

Castor — on how you look at it.

King Pelias (*interrupting the play*) Those actors don't look anything like each other?

Pollux Who said that!?

Castor Who said that!?

Pollux I'll slice 'em in two, Caz.

Castor Teach 'em a lesson, Pol.

Castor }
Pollux } (*together*) No one disses the Tyndarius twins.

King Pelias All right, move on, we get the idea.

Argrin arrives

Argrin Which of you is the rightful king of Greece?

All Argonauts (*to Jason*) That's you!

Jason Er — that would be me.

Argrin I am Argrin. My father Argo, the boat builder, sends you greetings. Our dads fought in battle together and although my dad is too sick to make the journey here today, he sends me to offer you our family's support in your quest to overthrow the tyrant Pelias. Your journey to the fleece will be a long one — you need a mighty ship. My father sends you such a vessel and if you will allow me to act as navigator I promise you as safe a journey as Neptune allows.

Jason I accept your kind offer. Crew, we have ourselves a ship and a navigator! May the gods bless the good ship Argo and all present and future.

All Argonauts (*shouting*) ARGONAUTS!

Hercules arrives

Hercules Excuse me, excuse me, excuse me, does anyone know anything about that ship over there? The Argo?

Argrin I built it, why?

Hercules I'm afraid I slipped and put my hand through the side.

Argrin But it's solid oak.

Hercules I know, sorry, this is always happening. Embarrassing really but I don't know my own strength. The name's Hercules. I'm looking for someone called Jason.

Jason That's me! So you're the legendary Hercules?

Hercules Well — don't know about legendary, strangled a few snakes with my bare hands when I was a baby. Cleaned out a few stables. People seem to get excited about it. Pleased to meet you. (*He holds out his hand*)

Jason high fives him instead, to avoid a hand crushing

Lovely boat!

Argrin It *was*.

Castor ⎫
Pollux ⎭ (*together*) We'll help you fix it up!

Hercules If you need me to rip up a tree for more wood — that's one of my things.

Jason You're going to be so useful. Take your place amongst the other Argonauts. Line up beside our identical twins.

Castor ⎫
Pollux ⎭ (*together*) That's us.

Hercules (*aside to Jason*) They don't look anything like each other.

Castor ⎫
Pollux ⎭ (*together; ready to fight*) Who said that?! Who said that?!

Jason Welcome! Welcome Hercules.

The gang disperse amongst the audience introducing members to Jason

Hercules Behold Captain! here is Bellerophon, the dragon slayer, he/she too would join your crew.

Castor Here's Mopsus, they say he/she can predict the weather.

Atlanta Hephaestus, blacksmith to the gods, is here. His/her arm is strong and true.

Argrin The Boreads clan can run as fast as the wind, an extraordinary family.

Pollux Can this be Euphemus? They say he/she walks on water when the mood takes him/or her.

Narcissus Here's my buddy Orpheus, love the new single, Bro!

Hercules Here is the trickster Autolycus, you won't believe what he can do with a cup, a ball of string and a squirrel.

Jason Welcome to all of you Argonauts. Now all we need is a cabin boy and a ship's cat.

Cat steps up. She speaks in a "gangsta" rapper style

Cat Yo, yo, yo! 'Sup Blood? What you pay, Mister?
Jason Sorry?
Cat I is a cat, you want a cat, I is a cat, you want a C to the A to the T, here I is, you pay Miss Kitty good though right?
Jason What did they give you on your last voyage?
Cat Respect! R-E-S-P-E-C-T. And 'T' is for tickle behind the ear which I get whenever I want. Access all areas and three fish heads a week.
Jason I'll make it four.
Cat Wicky wa wa. You got yourself a ship's cat, bruv!
Jason Great!
Cat Hush, hush now. Just one more thing yeah. Miss Kitty don't get no water on her fur! (*To the audience*) Any of you gets water on my fur, you is dead!

Medea rushes in followed by Chiron the Centaur

Medea Jason, Jason there you are. I heard about the ship, and the crew. Great news! I was worried I'd be late and you'd have to sail without me.
Narcissus This little lady coming too? Cool beans!
Argrin Captain Jason, I'm sorry but the boat can only safely carry a set number of Argonauts. Once we've recruited a cabin boy we're up to our limit — health and safety regulations.
Jason But May and I go everywhere together.
Medea We've never been parted.
Jason We're a team.
Medea You can't leave me behind. Who's going to hold your hand when things get scary or help you think of clever plans when the going's tough?
Chiron Medea, you will please stay here with me. You will help me prepare the kingdom for Jason as king. You can be of much help to me. It is your destiny. Will you do the courageous thing and trust in this role I have allotted you?
Medea Yeah, right! While everyone else goes off on an adventure without me?
Hera Loyal Medea, hear me speak. I am Hera, goddess and protector of women. I feel your pain at being separated from Jason. But I will watch over you both. I promise you will not be parted from your friend for long. My ways are mysterious. Will you accept my guidance?

Jason is transfixed by the beautiful Hera

Medea (*trying unsuccessfully to get Jason's attention back*) G'bye then, Jason.

Jason (*barely paying attention to Medea, still staring adoringly at Hera*) See ya, May.

Chiron escorts jealous Medea away

Jason (*to Hera*) Beautiful lady, we will do your every bidding but will you not sail with us?

Hera Hold me in your heart, Jason and I will not be far away. Your new friends will take care of you.

Storyteller And so the Argonauts set out on their perilous sea journey to fetch the Golden Fleece from Colchis. Some weeks later we find them, with empty stomachs, on the deck of the good ship Argo scouring the horizon for land.

Cat My gosh, Miss Kitty's hungry.

Argrin (*with a chart*) With the constellations to guide us we'll be in Colchis before the season turns.

Castor
Pollux } (*together*) We're off to swab the deck.

Cat (*annoyed at being ignored*) Excuse me! I said ——

Before Castor and Pollux can leave

Hercules Er... I think I just snapped my oar!

Castor
Pollux } (*together*) Not again!

Narcissus (*to Atlanta*) Hey babe, 'sup? So how about you and me sleep out on deck tonight and count the stars. (*Indicating himself*) Starting with this heavenly body.

Atlanta Well, gee, Mister... but I think I'd rather lay my head in a barrel of rattlesnakes.

Narcissus Chicks!

Atlanta And one of these days I'm gonna teach yah women ain't your feathered friends.

Everyone is still ignoring Cat

Cat My bruvas from plenty of other mothers, let's just get one thing straight right now yeah. When Miss Kitty speaks yeah you better listen right 'cause she got de weapons. (*She shows her claws*)

Castor
Pollux } (*together*) My identical twin is hungry!

Argrin Now you mention it, where is Canthus the cabin boy, with the elevenses?

Narcissus (*to Atlanta*) Wow! Baby, the way those beautiful eyes are flashing sets me on fire.

Cat (*frustrated at being ignored*) People!? Hallo!

Argrin (*to Narcissus*) Can I suggest you douse yourself with a cold shower.

Atlanta Well, I sure am ready for a chow. I've climbed up and down them sails twenty times this morning.

Hercules How about I jump overboard and wrestle some sharks on to the deck. We could have shark sandwiches.

Everyone groans

Castor }
Pollux } (*together*) Again!

Narcissus I say the ladies go down to the galley and work a little feminine culinary magic.

Cat (*referring to Hercules*) Wait, wait, I like his plan with a big fish better.

Atlanta (*to Narcissus*) And why can't *you* do some cooking?

Narcissus No way. I'm not going near them supplies, that cabin boy is mean.

Cat digs her claws into Hercules' behind

Hercules Argh! That cat just clawed my bottom.

Cat Big fish! Catch the big fish. Miss Kitty, she hungry!

Medea disguised as Canthus the cabin boy arrives

Medea There are no fish around here, it's too salty for them to survive — this is a dead sea.

Argrin (*looking at the chart; surprised*) He's right, you're quite correct, cabin boy. It says so on the chart.

Atlanta Clever little guy ain't yah, Canthus? Handsome young thing too!

Cat So what you telling Kitty here rough t'ing, there ain't going to be no fish to eat?!

Medea There are no fish to catch and you've eaten all the supplies. I warned you all not to eat everything at once.

Castor }
Pollux } (*together*) But, Canthus, my brother is starving!

Narcissus We all are.
Hercules Where's Jason?
Castor Writing love poetry.
Pollux Again!
Narcissus He's really got it bad for that chick he left behind.
Medea Really?
Narcissus I don't know, I'm too hungry to think.
Hercules How am I supposed to keep my strength up?
Atlanta Couldn't you just fry us up some beans?
Medea There's not a bean left, nothing. Just one last fish head.

Cat sidles up to Medea

Cat (*aside*) Girlfriend, may I strongly suggest you wanna keep that for
  Miss Kitty?
Medea (*aside*) Why?
Cat (*aside*) 'Cause, she heard you praying to your home girl the
  goddess, Hera, last night. You ain't no cabin boy. You're that crazy
  Medea chick in disguise.
Medea (*aside*) Don't tell anyone.
Cat (*aside*) Don't fret, pet. Miss Kitty don't like to chitter chatter.
  Particularly after a good meal, yeah?
Medea (*aside*) Oh, all right you can have the last fish head.
Cat (*aside*) Nuff respect, girl. In that case your secret is well safe with
  me. Sounds like your man Jason's got it bad for you girl. When you
  going to tell him you tricked your way aboard?
Medea (*aside*) As soon as I know he won't be cross.
Hercules (*interrupting their private conversation*) So what are we
  going to do? How will we survive without food?
Castor } (*together; indicating each other*) { I'm fine. It's him I'm
Pollux }   { worried about.
Atlanta Maybe we'll pitch up somewhere soon.
Argrin The map is very vague for this area. It's not clear when we'll
  reach the next island.
Jason Land ahoy! (*Rushing in*) Argonauts! There's an island appeared
  on the horizon.
Hercules Great, Boss. We can pick up some fresh supplies.
Argrin I'm not sure about this. According to the chart there shouldn't
  be an island in these waters.
Castor } (*together*) We see it too!
Pollux }
Castor My brother and I ——
Pollux —— would like to volunteer for the landing party.

Jason Very well, prepare the rowing boat. Hercules, your strength at the oars will be invaluable if we need a quick getaway. Narcissus, fetch some gold from the store as an offering to the island. Cabin Boy, list the supplies we need from them. Everyone else guard the ship, we will be back with food before nightfall.

All Argonauts Aye aye, Captain!

Storyteller And so the little rowing boat set off from the good ship Argo with our plucky heroes aboard. The island was welcoming with gentle slopes cascading down the hillside from the castle and soon the Argonauts stood at its door.

Jason mimes pushing a doorbell. Traditional two-tone doorbell sound

A lascivious old Crone opens the door. All this can be mimed with silly sound effects

Crone Yes — who is it? (*Seeing Jason*) Oooh hallo, ducks.

Jason Greetings, Keeper of the Gates.

Crone Oooh, aren't you lovely? (*Calling over her shoulder*) Oooh Joan! You should come and see what's just turned up. (*To Jason*) Aren't you a hunk? (*To off*) Joan, He's absolutely gorrrrrrgeous!

Jason I am Jason of Jason and the Argonauts!

Crone Ooooh, lovely. D'you know, you've a look of that Daniel Craigicus?

Jason Thank you. My friends and I ——

Crone Brought some friends, have you? Let's have a look at 'em. (*Inspecting them short-sightedly*) Oooh lovely. Such well-turned thighs and pert buttocks. You're all gorrrrgeous! We don't see a lot of men here in Lemnos. The queen will be ever so pleased you've come.

Jason Please send my regards to your mistress and inform her that we'd like to buy some food. Our provisions have run low.

Crone Oh, where are my manners? Of course we must get you something to eat. What are you like, big boy, distracting me by being so gorrrrgeous? Come in. Come in. (*Calling*) Girls! Come and meet the boys — fresh supplies off the boat.

Sexy girls enter. These can be played by male and female performers in long blonde wigs

Narcissus Wow! Babelicious!

All Girls Gorrrrrgeous!

Crone Fetch the queen.

Jason Fair ladies, allow me to introduce my cabin boy and some of my crew — Narcissus, Hercules and the identical twins Castor and Pollux.

Girl (*aside to a friend*) They look nothing like each other!

Castor } (*together*) Who said that?
Pollux }

Crone Where's your manners girls? Give the visitors some wine while they wait for their food!

Medea sneaks away and watches

Queen Callisto arrives

Crone Your Majesty.

Queen Callisto Well done, Nursey. The wine should keep them sedated until we work out what to do with them.

Crone (*of Jason*) I know what I'd like to do with that one. He's gorrrrrgeous.

Queen Callisto Nursey! Aren't we forgetting something?

Crone What's that, popsykins?

Queen Callisto Remember, Nursey — men are beasts.

Optional girl power pop song can be inserted here introduced by the line "We don't need 'em. Sing it with me our kid!"

Girls, throw off your disguises, it's time to show the world our true selves.

During the next speech, the women put on masks to become Harpies

Storyteller At that moment a cloud covered the moon, a wind whipped through the palace and the beautiful maidens were transformed into Harpies, terrible half-bird, half-woman creatures.

Queen Callisto The food is ours and ours alone! Peck out their eyes, girls! And poop in the sockets!

Medea steps in

Medea Stop! Wait! Jason! Wake up! Hercules, Castor, Pollux, Narcissus!

Jason What's going on?

Hercules Ooh my head!

Castor That was powerful wine!

Pollux You never know when we've had enough!

Medea Captain, we're in terrible danger!

Jason Harpies!

The boys spring up with swords drawn

Hercules Whatsies?

Jason I've seen pictures of them on a vase. Men are their sworn enemies.

Narcissus Hey! Where did the babes go?

Jason (*aside to the men*) It's them. This is how the Harpies always looked underneath?

Narcissus Girls, girls! Time to refresh the make-up.

Queen Callisto For a man, never!

Narcissus And what's so bad about us guys?

Queen Callisto Unfeeling brutes, your only thought is to enslave us, chain us to the kitchen, confine us to the bedroom. We will not be conquered.

Narcissus Whoa, whoa, whoa there, cream puff! Not all men are like that. Take our captain Jason here.

Hercules ⎫
Castor ⎬ (*together*) Yeah, take him!
Pollux ⎭

Narcissus His lady's got him all tied up in knots. Read 'em your poem, Jase.

Music out

Jason What? Now...? I couldn't... It's not very good.

Narcissus But it's from the heart. Show these fine ladies how you feel about your girl, that we aren't all cavemen.

Jason Um... well. (*He unfolds the poem and quotes the lyrics of a favourite pop ballad, reading them clumsily so it sounds like bad poetry*)

Narcissus Jase, Jase! You're not going to get yourself a girlfriend like that. Let me give it a little Narcissus magic. Ladies, listen up. Do these sound like the words of a brute to you?

Queen Callisto No, it's rubbish. C'mon, girls, let's kill 'em!

Narcissus takes the lyrics and sings them to a karaoke track, as a pop star, in the way they're intended to be performed

The Harpies behave like hysterical teenage fans

Narcissus finishes

Queen Callisto (*kittenish now*) You're right, the words do have a certain charm.

Crone Gorrrrrrgeous!

Queen Callisto Very well, you may be on your way. But on one condition. (*Indicating Narcissus*) Leave him behind.

Jason Narcissus?

Narcissus Baby, I can't disappoint a bird, can I? You know me, never resist the chicks. Peck me up on the way back.

Jason Very well, good luck.

The men gather to wish Narcissus luck whilst the Queen Callisto takes Medea to one side

Queen Callisto What about you, girl? That disguise doesn't fool me. Can we persuade you to stay?

Medea I have to look after Jason.

Queen Callisto I thought I recognized a love sick look in your eye. He'll be trouble that one, I can tell. I hope you're prepared to see off plenty of rivals. (*Pressing a small bottle into Medea's hand*) Take this potion, and if another steals his heart, a few drops of it on her gown or in her hair will melt her flesh like treacle. See who's prettier then, eh?

Medea (*appalled*) That's horrible. (*She stares at the bottle in horror*)

Queen Callisto (*ignoring her; to Jason*) We will ensure your ship has everything you need for your voyage. How far do you travel?

Jason Thank you, Your Majesty. (*To Medea who still stares at the bottle*) What's that, Canthus? Medicine? (*To Queen Callisto*) We sail for Colchis, home of the Golden Fleece.

Queen Callisto Colchis? The island at the end of the world. Great peril awaits you on that voyage.

Medea pockets the bottle

Sail North West until you pass the straits of Epimetheus. Then turn eastward and sail for a day until you reach Symplegades, the Clashing Rocks.

Castor
Pollux } (*together*) Clashing Rocks!

Queen Callisto Colchis awaits you through the narrow opening. But beware these rocks smash together and crush ships to matchwood. Few survive! Oh well, have fun. Send us a postcard. Ta-ra!

Storyteller (*to King Pelias*) And so, Your Majesty, with Queen Callisto's warning ringing in the Argonauts' ears, they returned to the good ship Argo and set sail in trepidation, as she had instructed them. Word of the impending danger soon spread amongst the crew.

Cat (*to Argrin*) Let me get this straight, homey. We're heading for crashing what?

Argrin Rocks. They're very big apparently. At least two hundred feet high and if any ship tries to sail through them they sort of... (*weakly*) crash together. (*Miming this by bringing hands together*) Crash.

Cat Show me that move again.

Argrin (*repeating hand gesture*) Crash.

Cat (*copying*) Crash. Let me explain it to you once. Miss Kitty don't do no "crash". 'Cause "crash" means the boat go "crunch" and then it sinks and Miss Kitty get wet. AND MISS KITTY DOES NOT GET WET!

Castor ⎫
Pollux ⎭ (*together*) My brother's not very happy about it either.

Hercules It's definitely a bit of a downer.

Medea Listen to you all! Don't you think Jason has a plan? He wouldn't have brought us all this way just to be crushed between a couple of old rocks. He'll know what to do.

Hercules Of course he will. He'll know what to do.

Castor ⎫
Pollux ⎭ (*together*) We have every confidence in him.

Argrin He's got us this far.

Cat I don't know, he never struck me as that bright before. Seems like the kinda bloke that wouldn't even know his own girlfriend if she turned up in disguise.

Medea stands on her tail

Ow! You did not just stand on my tail though!?

Medea takes Cat to one side. The others disperse

Medea You promised not to tell anyone.

Cat Easy child, Miss Kitty's just thinking you might need a helping hand. Your man's forgotten all about you.

Medea He has not, didn't you hear about the poem he wrote me? Narcissus charmed the Harpies with it.

Cat What makes you think that poem was about you?

Medea Well, of course it was about me. Who else would it be for?

Jason appears and interrupts them

Jason Canthus?

Medea Yes, Captain Jason.

Jason How is morale amongst the Argonauts?

Medea I think they're all very worried about the Clashing Rocks, Sir.

Jason I need to inspire them, Canthus. What should I say? If Medea were here she'd have the right words. (*Sighing*) If only I could get her out of my mind.

Romantic underscore starts

Medea The philosophers tell us that love is the most powerful force in the universe, Captain. All the great heroes have fallen under its spell.
Jason Have the philosophers any tips for winning the heart of a goddess?
Medea (*flattered*) Aw… come on now… I hear Medea's pretty cool but she's not a goddess.
Jason May? A goddess, that's funny… She'd laugh at that. She's my best mate but probably a good idea she stayed behind, don't you reckon? This voyage is a bit a scary for her. Do you think my goddess knows how much I love her?
Medea Just a minute! Your "goddess". Who are you talking about?
Jason The goddess Hera, of course.

The romantic music cuts out

Medea Hera! You're in love with Hera?
Jason From the moment I saw her I knew she was the one for me.
Medea You're not in love with Medea?
Jason May? No! Not in that way. She's like my kid sister. Well, I'd better go and think about how to inspire the crew. I'm sure Hera will help us. (*Sighing*) What a babe…

Jason leaves US

Cat looks at Medea

Cat Gutted. Know what I'm saying though.
Medea He doesn't love me at all!

The goddess Hera appears

Hera Not yet, my child. But he will. The Gods have decreed your futures are linked, your hearts will join as one and you will have children together.
Medea It doesn't sound that way. Did you hear him, he thinks of me like a kid sister! How can I compete with you?
Hera It's true my beauty is beyond compare but perhaps our friend here (*indicating Cat*) can assist you with a makeover.

Cat That's gonna take a lot of product.

Hera Mortal love is not for me. All men realize that in time. I will release Jason's heart when you are worthy to receive it and he can recognize you as his equal in bravery and honour.

Medea I can't believe he thinks I'd be scared.

Hera You must prove him wrong with a brilliant act of valour that will establish you as his worthy partner.

Medea How do I do that?

Hera You must save this ship and all the Argonauts from the Clashing Rocks.

Medea What? But I…

Hera If you truly love him, you will find a way. Goodbye for now, good luck my friend.

Hera exits

Medea Wait, don't leave me alone.

Cat Miss Kitty, not good enough for you?

Medea Oh, I'm sure you mean well... but how can a cat help?

Cat She can help plenty, if she's really a goddess.

Medea You're a goddess?

Cat (*speaking more formally now*) Allow me to formally introduce myself. I am the goddess Artemis, goddess of animals, my father Zeus sent me to watch over you, disguised as a cat. He said you two might need a hand getting together. Destiny has designs for the two of you.

Medea But you heard Hera, I have to find a way to stop the Argo being crushed.

Cat I've heard the rocks spring apart again once they've slammed together. If you could swim through alone triggering them to clash, the Argonauts could row quickly through as they opened up again behind you.

Medea But I'd be smashed to pieces.

Cat But if you were small and light and fast… I could turn you into a wild salmon, or an eel or a dolphin… No, the strong currents would pull you back. I have it! You won't swim through — you could — it's still very dangerous, you'll need all your strength and courage but — with my help — you could fly!

Jason comes forward to address the crew

Medea and Cat withdraw

Jason Argonauts, I've had dream. The goddess Artemis appeared before me. She is sending a dove, a brave little dove, to fly through the rocks before us triggering both sides to smash together. As the rocks open up again we will row as fast as we can between them. If we are fast enough we will pass through before we're detected. Just a moment. Where is Canthus?

Hercules No one's seen the cabin boy, Captain. Or the cat.

Atlanta What if we can't row fast enough?

Castor }
Pollux } (*together*) We could be squished.

Argrin I'm not sure I'm brave enough.

Atlanta It doesn't look like we'll even reach the Golden Fleece.

Pollux What a way to end our days.

Argrin We'll never see home again.

Jason I won't blame any of you if you want to take the rowing boat and head for home. But I must go on.

The action freezes

Artemis and Hera meet. Celestial-type underscore

Hera (*to Artemis*) Hail, Goddess of animals.

Artemis (*to Hera*) Hail, Goddess of women. What do you have there, sister?

Hera Jason's shoe, I caught it just now as it fell from the crow's nest where Jason had climbed to keep watch.

Artemis Don't ancient prophesies foretell that a shoeless hero will avenge a father's death and save his country?

Hera They do. If he can also earn the love of a brave young woman.

Artemis Then everything goes to plan, sister?

Hera Everything goes to plan.

The Jason action unfreezes. Celestial music cuts out

A dove, a puppet operated by Medea, flies to Jason. This can be Medea wearing white gloves linking her thumbs to make a bird shape with her hands

Jason Are you the brave little dove that will lead us to freedom? Good luck little bird. Fly strong and fast and we'll see you on the other side. See you in Colchis everyone… (*Low key*) Or with our ancestors in the afterlife.

Tension music pulses

Medea now holds up the puppet dove. Ahead of her and to either side, the Argonauts hold up a wall of grey beach umbrellas to represent the two walls of rock

Storyteller Poor Medea! She seemed so tiny transformed into a dove, riding the air currents high above the mighty waves. She focused on the treacherous ravine. She must fly through knowing full well those mighty cliff walls could smash her to smithereens. Then, with her heart pounding in her tiny snow white breast, she flapped her wings and flew as no bird has flown before!

Medea passes through the umbrellas and they begin to close behind her

The Argonauts bring down the umbrellas and reform staring out front as if on the deck of the ship looking out after the dove

Atlanta Did she make it?
Argrin (*with a telescope*) I don't know. I can't see.
Jason Mighty Apollo, we pray so. But come on, gang. No time to hang about. When the rocks start to open we must row as never before.

They resume their positions as the umbrella-rocks

The Storyteller stands before them holding up a shoe to represent the Argo. She turns it to point the toe towards the rocks

Storyteller The brave Argonauts pointed the Argo towards the treacherous causeway and prepared to row through like demons as the rocks moved slowly apart.

King Pelias fights his way through the umbrellas and, interrupting the play, addresses the Storyteller

King Pelias (*indicating the shoe*) Just a minute. What, pray, is that?
Storyteller It is the mighty ship Argo, Your Majesty, crammed with anxious Argonauts preparing to row for their lives through the treacherous rocks that guard passage to Colchis.
King Pelias (*referring to Jason*) It's that boy's smelly lost shoe.
Storyteller Well, yes, Majesty but through the magic of storytelling I have transformed it into ——
King Pelias Yes, I'm aware of the conventions of physical theatre, thank you. It's just you're playing the palace now, love, not school assembly. I think we can do a little better than that! (*He claps his hands*)

A beautiful model of the Argo is passed to the Storyteller. Everyone admires it as she holds it up

Back to the action

Jason   Row like you have never rowed before.

The model boat ends up going round in circles. The Argonauts reform to represent the crew rowing. The closed umbrellas become oars

Castor   What's going on?
Pollux   We're going round in circles.
Argrin   It's Hercules. He's rowing so hard. The oarsman on the other side can't keep up.
Jason   Quickly! Hercules, keep rowing on that side. Everyone else on the other.

They reconfigure. The boat moves forward

Atlanta   It's worked! We're moving forward again!
All Argonauts   HOORAY!

The Argonauts chant a sea shanty or boatman's song as they mime rowing until...

Jason   We made it!
All Argonauts   Yay!
Storyteller   But had poor Medea been as lucky?

The actors disperse to reveal Medea apparently washed up dead on the beach

Hera and Cat/Artemis appear and look down at her

Hera (*to Artemis*) Sister!
Artemis (*to Hera*) Sister! (*Referring to Medea*) Is she dead?
Hera   Not quite, but the life breath is shallow, her lungs struggle from her exertions.
Artemis   That is why I have changed her back from dove to human form. She will be stronger this way.
Hera   And Jason will find her.
Artemis   The Argonauts have landed further up the coast.
Hera   So there will be a romantic reunion.

Artemis Not yet. We are too late, a fisherman's wife has spotted the body washed up on the shore.

A Fishwife looks down at Medea

Fishwife (*speaking identically to the lasivious Crone from earlier*) Ooh look at you, you're gorrrrgeous. (*Calling off*) Joan! Joan! Come and have a look at this dead girl the tide's washed up… she's gorrrrgeous!

Medea (*stirring*) Where am I? Who are you?

Fishwife Alive are you, dearie? That's nice but you'd better not hang about. The King likes to walk this way of a morning to check the horizon for invaders. Where do you come from? How did you get here?

Medea Long story, I used to be a dove.

Fishwife Oooh gorgeous! But you can't be lying here when the King arrives. (*Spotting something in the distance*) Oh dear, too late.

The Fishwife moves to hide Medea

Artemis (*to Hera*) Who is ruler of Colchis?

Hera (*to Artemis*) The mighty and noble King Aeetes.

King Pelias (*interrupting the play*) Mighty? Noble? Cousin Titties? Ill-bred, ill-mannered little squirt more like. Still, he kept those meatheads, Jason and Dove Girl, from the Golden Fleece, eh?

King Aeetes, a sleazy and uninspiring figure, enters

Fishwife Good morning, Your Majesty.

King Aeetes Morning, fisherwoman. Lovely day again.

Fishwife (*standing in front of Medea*) I know. Isn't it gorrrrgeous!

King Aeetes (*indicating Medea*) Are you hiding something there?

Fishwife Oh, it's nothing, Your Majesty. It's just a dead dove.

King Aeetes A dead dove?

Fishwife Yes, belonged to me deaf, dead dad.

King Aeetes Your deaf, dead dad?

Fishwife Yes, dear. (*Stepping aside, revealing Medea*) It's just Dan Dod my deaf, dead dad's dead dove. As you might say.

King Aeetes I'd rather not. It looks like my troublesome daughter to me. I thought we'd seen the last of her when I packed her off to Athens. Guards! Take my daughter up to her room and make sure she stays there.

Guards drag away the drowsy Medea

(*To the Fishwife*) And as for you... as for you? We will hear no more of your dead, deaf dad, Dan Dod's, dead dove. I've a good mind to have you thrown into the dungeons.

Fishwife Chuck me in chains in a chilly chamber?

King Aeetes Don't start that again!

Jason and the crew approach

Jason Greetings King Aeetes, I am Captain Jason of the Argonauts!

Fishwife He's gorrrrrgeous!

King Aeetes (*to Fishwife*) Silence! (*To Jason*) Welcome travellers. Visitors usually get squished by the rocks so it's a particular pleasure to meet you.

Jason We would ask a favour, mighty King.

King Pelias Mighty King?

King Aeetes I'll help if I can.

Jason I must beg the Golden Fleece from you. If I return home with it I shall be declared king.

King Aeetes Oh lovely, wouldn't that be lovely. Lovely to be king. (*Musing*) Give you the Golden Fleece, give you the Golden Fleece... now let me see... NO!

Jason No?

King Aeetes You can't just beg an ancient artefact like the Fleece. You must earn it as befits a hero. Up to the job?

Jason I'll try sir. I was top of my class at Hero Training School.

King Aeetes Our life here is simple, we are poor farmers. Your challenge will be an agricultural one.

Jason I'll be happy to oblige, sir. Where are the oxen?

King Aeetes You'll just need the one beast. (*Ordering*) Send for the mighty Bull of Colchis! You may find him a bit of a handful.

Jason I believe if you treat all animals with kindness they will respect you in return. How bad tempered is he?

King Aeetes It's not so much the bad temper as the razor sharp golden hooves that can kick a man in half, in an instant.

Jason I shall stay away from those hooves.

King Aeetes And his breath of course.

Jason His breath.

King Aeetes He breathes fire.

There is a mighty roar from off stage

King Aeetes Good luck persuading him to draw the plough. Here are the seeds you must plant to win the fleece. Nice knowing you!

A servant deposits a sack of seeds

Another roar and the gigantic, fire-breathing bull stands before Jason who is scared

Jason O Great Bull of Colchis I salute you.

The Bull is very depressed, an Eeyore-type creature

Great Bull You can call me Bugsy if you like. Not that it matters, I'm going to fry you with my breath anyway. Or kick you to pieces. I'm not sure which. Not that it matters. Nothing matters much.
Jason Why do you say that? Why does nothing matter?
Great Bull Bugsy.
Jason Bugsy.
Great Bull Do you know? No one's ever asked me that before. Not that it matters. Right, it's time to barbecue you on my breath. Ready? Not that it matters.
Jason It must be painful to have such fire in your belly, Bugsy.
Great Bull Got indigestion like you wouldn't believe, son.
Jason Is it spicy food that puts fire on your breath?
Great Bull I don't know what it is, to be honest. These days I'm mostly vegetarian since this tooth started giving me grief! (*Wincing*) Ouch! It hurts. See, you've got me all worked up now and my toothache's come back. Prepare to poach!

Medea comes back on to the stage with her sword drawn

Medea The next guard to lay a finger on me will feel this sword in their belly. (*Turning to find herself face to face with Jason*) Jason!
Jason May!

Artemis appears and incants

Artemis   Now it's time for love to wake,
                     Relationships can new forms take.
                     Friendship blossoms, turns to more;
                     Romance, passion, what's in store?
                     For now he loves as she loves him,
                     The fire inside them will not dim.

Jason Medea? How did you get here? I've… I've missed you.

Medea I've missed you too. (*Business-like again*) Never mind that now. They tell me you're in great danger. No one has ever tamed the Great Bull of Colchis.

Great Bull Thank you. I was beginning to feel ignored! That's not a good feeling when you've got the toothache.

Jason Just a moment. If I were to take a look in your mouth and see if I could make you more comfortable would you refrain from kicking me to death?

Great Bull Worth a try I suppose. Not making any promises. Not that it matters. My advice would be — keep your distance.

Medea I think I can see the tooth is rotten. It's the infection that makes your breath fiery.

Great Bull No wonder I can't get dates with nice cows.

Jason I can help you but you mustn't kick, Bugsy. Do you promise not to kick?

Great Bull I'll try.

Jason Let me take a look.

Atlanta has been watching

Atlanta Captain Jason, would my lasso be of use? It's brought plenty of wild horses into line. I bet it could take care of a troublesome tooth.

Jason Thank you, Atlanta. (*Approaching the Bull's mouth and tying the lasso round the tooth*) We'll have that rotten tooth out in no time and your breath will soon be spring fresh. Now if I can just yank it out. Stand back everyone. Bugsy may kick out with his hooves! (*He pulls*)

Maybe a child from the audience helps too

The tooth comes out and the Bull roars!

Jason Calm down, Bugsy. Easy boy!

Great Bull Easy? Easy? I've just had half my mouth ripped out!

A vision of Hera disguised as a hag appears

Hera Remember, Jason, remember the wisdom of Old Mother Superdrug. Look in your bag ya great dafty!

Medea (*looking in Jason's bag*) Jason, look. It's the lotion of cloves she sold us. Be brave, Bugsy. (*She tentatively approaches the Bull and massages lotion into his gum*)

Great Bull (*purring with pleasure*) Jason, mate, she's a keeper.

Jason Do you know where we can find the Golden Fleece?

Great Bull Maybe if we plough the field it'll all become clear.

Medea (*looking at the seeds*) What are these seeds anyway? They look like little fangs. (*Reading on the sack*) "Thanatos Velarian".

Storyteller And so Jason harnessed the mighty bull——

Great Bull It's Bugsy!

Storyteller And so Jason harnessed Bugsy to the plough. Man and beast toiled together in the hot sun and by supper time they had sown all the sharp pointy seeds into the ground.

The Bull and Jason slump. Medea is reading a book and pacing

Jason I'm exhausted.

Great Bull Mind if I take a leak?

Jason Be my guest.

Medea (*finding what she's looking for in the book*) Here it is. "Thanatos" I knew I'd heard that before. It's the ancient word for the dead. "Velarian" means flower of course… You've planted Flowers of Death!

Jason Wonder what they can be?

Medea Let's not stick around to find out. I wouldn't want to be here when the rain makes them shoot.

Great Bull I'm bursting for a pee. Excuse me everyone.

Medea No — don't get the seeds wet!

The Bull starts to pee. A jet of water squirts everywhere maybe even the audience

Storyteller As moisture seeped into the ground, an army of skeletons sprang up around our heroes sending the terrified Bull fleeing to his stable and the Argonauts to Jason's side.

A sound effect of lots of skeletons giggling can be heard

The crew stare out front at the skeleton army confronting them

Atlanta There must be hundreds of the boney critters!

We hear the skeletons singing "We Ain't Got Nobody!"

Castor Fear not, Jason. The twins will not leave your side.

Pollux We shall fight as one, just as we look as one.

Hercules Courage, Argonauts. Hercules has never lost a battle yet. I shall slit their throats!

Medea Er — excuse me! In case you haven't noticed, you meathead, they're skeletons. They don't have throats.

Hercules I'll run them through the heart!

Medea Look again, big boy.

Hercules (*weakly*) Slice their gizzards!

Medea This will take brains not brute force.

Hercules (*to Jason; of Medea*) Who's she? Kind of familiar. (*To Medea*) You haven't got a cousin who's a cabin boy, have you?

Jason Hercules, guard the rear. Spread out everyone, good luck!

Storyteller And so the fearless Argonauts advanced on their enemy. Scattering the dry old bones into the dust.

Jason Watch out, Hercules, man on! On ya head!

A TV football theme plays

> *The performers, having skulls on the end of long sticks, enter and now thrust them at Hercules who fends them off, in slow motion, as if they were footballs. As he appears to kick or head a skull the performer at the other end of the stick sends it up and away. After a short time there are no more skulls left and Hercules is triumphant*

Storyteller Was there ever a more glorious victory for an Athens FC apprentice?!

With appropriate grand music, the Golden Fleece appears spectacularly US

Atlanta Look, Captain... that must be...

Hercules It must be…

Castor }
Pollux } (*together*) We both think there's every chance that's...

Medea It is! It's the Golden Fleece, Jason. You alone can claim it.

Argrin Be careful, Captain, it could be booby trapped. And don't whatever you do try it on. I hear it'll melt your skin away!

Jason We've come too far for me to chicken out now.

Medea Good luck, Jase.

The others all back away as Jason approaches the Golden Fleece

> *A gigantic Dragon Snake appears*

Dragon Snake Not sssssssssso fasssssssst, pretty boy!

Jason Who are you?

Dragon Snake I am the Dragon Snake who guards the Golden Fleece. Thought you could sneak past me, did you? Well, you were wrong. No one getsssss passst me. My eyelids have been ssssssewn open!

Jason Really. How long have you been this way?

Dragon Snake How long… how long… I've never really thought. A thousand… maybe two thoussssand years. Why? What's it to you?

Medea steps in and intercedes

Medea My friend was just thinking — if your eyes have been open for thousands of years you must be very sleepy?

Dragon Snake Sleepy? Sleepy? I don't think sssssssssssso. I learnt my lesson a long time ago back in Athens when as a baby I fell asleep in a basket. That fool Phrixus didn't noticed me amongst his provisions and carried me here on the back of his flying ram.

Jason Hang on. You're from Athens? Us too.

Dragon Snake Lovely, you'll taste of home.

Medea But don't you ever get homesick?

Dragon Snake Don't you?

Medea Yes, but every night I can return in my dreams. Try it. I have a pot of soothing balm, I could massage your forehead. Let my friends sing you a lullaby, drift away and imagine going home to Athens. It's almost like being there.

Jason sings gently. Tune: "Show Me The Way To Go Home"

The other Argonauts appear and hum along gently

Soon the Dragon Snake is fast asleep. Jason pulls on some surgical gloves so he can touch the fleece

Jason (*collecting the fleece*) I'll return it one day I promise, Snakey. How about it gang!? Ready for the voyage back?! It's time for me to take my rightful place as king.

King Pelias climbs down from his throne. The company surrounds him

King Pelias I don't understand. You told me an hour ago that Jason hadn't escaped the Dragon Snake. Are you saying…? Are you telling me…? (*To the company*) Who are you all!?

Jason I am Jason, of Jason and the Argonauts. You stole my father's crown. Surrender it to me so I may rule justly and in his memory.

Ceremoniously, the reluctant King Pelias kneels and presents the crown from his head to Jason, as the Argonauts sing, big and hymn-like, "Show Me The Way To Go Home"

Big musical finish as Jason puts on the crown. The Argonauts repeat the 5th and 6th lines of "Show Me The Way To Go Home"

Jason Medea, will you marry me? Together we can rule wisely and compassionately, as my father would have wished.

They kiss. Everyone cheers, then sings the final two lines of "Show Me The Way To Go Home"

Up tempo — all singing, all dancing — curtain call to a medley of the pop hits used in the show

THE END

FURNITURE AND PROPERTY LIST

On stage: Throne
Box

Off stage: Recorder (**Robbie**)
Crown (**An actor**)
Pictures on flip chart (**Herald**)
Tray of medicines (**Hera**)
Groats (**Jason**)
Cup of tea (**An actor**)
Masks (**Harpies**)
Poem (**Jason**)
Small bottle (**Queen Callisto**)
Dove puppet (**Medea**)
Beach umbrellas (**Argonauts**)
Telescope (**Argrin**)
Shoe (**Storyteller**)
Model boat (**An actor**)
Sack of seeds (**Servant**)
Book (**Medea**)
Skulls on the end of long sticks (**Performers**)
Golden Fleece

Personal: **Argonauts**: swords
Bull: tooth
Jason: bag. *In it:* massage lotion, surgical gloves
King Pelias: crown

LIGHTING PLOT

Practical fitting required: nil
1 interior. The same scene throughout

To open: General lighting

No cues

EFFECTS PLOT

Cue 1	**Chiron**: "That wouldn't be too difficult." *Training music starts*	(Page 4)
Cue 2	**King Pelias**: "...the Golden Fleece of Colchis!" *A drum beats to accompany the challenge*	(Page 5)
Cue 3	**Hera**: "What lies in store for these two crazy kids?" *Thunder clap*	(Page 7)
Cue 4	**King Pelias**: "...my youngest daughter Alcestis." *Vampy music*	(Page 8)
Cue 5	**Jason** mimes pushing a door bell *Traditional two-tone doorbell sound*	(Page 16)
Cue 6	**Crone** opens the door *Silly sound effects*	(Page 16)
Cue 7	**Queen Callisto**: "Remember, Nursey—men are beasts." *Girl power pop song (optional)*	(Page 17)
Cue 8	**Narcissus**: "Read 'em your poem, Jase." *Music out*	(Page 18)
Cue 9	**Narcissus** sings the lyrics *Karaoke track plays*	(Page 18)
Cue 10	**Jason**: "...out of my mind." *Romantic underscore starts*	(Page 21)
Cue 11	**Jason**: "The goddess Hera, of course." *Romantic music cuts out*	(Page 21)
Cue 12	**Artemis** and **Hera** meet *Celestial-type underscore*	(Page 23)
Cue 13	The Jason action unfreezes *Celestial music cuts out*	(Page 23)

Printed in the United Kingdom by Hobbs the Printers Ltd, Totton, Hampshire